DEATH INTO LIFE

F. J. SHEED

DEATH
INTO
LIFE

A Conversation

PHOTOGRAPHS BY CATHARINE HUGHES

Arena Lettres   New York

Nihil Obstat: Rev. Francis A. DeDomenico, S.T.L.
Censor Librorum

Imprimatur: ✠ Peter L. Gerety, D.D.
Archbishop of Newark

Date: September 27, 1977

DEATH INTO LIFE

Printed in the United States of America

Library of Congress Catalog Card No. 77-85417

ISBN: 0-88479-005-3

Contents

Preface   vii

Survival   1

The Mind of Christ   25

Refusal   37

Acceptance, But—   69

Maturity   89

A Reflection   131

v

Preface

Do men revere great Shakespeare's name?
To Shakespeare it is all the same.
Is Danton's memory detested?
Well, Danton isn't interested.
What praise or blame, what cheers or groans
Affect a buried box of bones?

So wrote a verse-maker of my Australian boyhood. I thought it entertaining, but did not find my faith affected in the slightest. There is a pleasure in seeing views one doesn't hold stated forcefully.

In the long course of my grown-up life I have had hundreds of dialogues on what follows death—at dinner tables, on trains and planes, at university conferences, in London's Hyde Park, in New York's Times Square and Sydney's Domain, with militant atheists, with bothered believers.

What follows is in the form of a dialogue, a conversation. All the questions and objections I give actually were said to me, though not by the same person, of course. What you read here is a composite of all those dialogues—and indeed of thousands of others. There can hardly be a believer anywhere who has not been involved in many such, if only with himself.

It may be worth mentioning that these are conversations, not arguments. As Cardinal Newman said, it would be as pointless to argue a man into belief as to torture him into it. In matters of this importance it would be folly to expect a few sentences to bring conviction. All we can hope is that the other parties to the conversation may give their full mind both to what we are saying and to what it might mean for them.

SURVIVAL

There has been a lot written recently about people who have been declared clinically dead but returned to life and what they say happened to them in the interval. I imagine you think that supports your case for an afterlife.

Not really. I have read the experiences they recount of the self leaving the body and of observing it from outside; of the not-quite body that they feel attached to the separate self, the dark tunnel, the light welcoming them, the meeting with friends, the reluctance to return to the body.

I find it fascinating. Much of it fits well enough with Christ's revelation. But, after all, it would seem that they were not *really* dead. One can conceive all sorts of changes in people who have stopped breathing, whose hearts have stopped beating—strange things happen in people whose hearts *are* beating. But I shall continue to read what gets written.

3

When you're dead, you're dead. How long will you people go on kidding yourselves about another life?

The number of those whom the questioner dismisses so slightingly as "you people" is enormous—over the whole span of history and still today. Among Christians, Hindus, Buddhists and Mohammedans—to say nothing of ancient Egyptians and American Indians—we find the belief that all is not ended when the body rots to corruption. "It's their delusion," says the objector. It might be worth his while and ours to wonder how so improbable a delusion became so widespread.

On one point we agree with him: a dead man looks so very dead. Why have all these people clung so tenaciously to the belief that death is not the end? We cannot answer for Mohammedans or Hindus or Ancient Egyptians or American Indians. But for ourselves we *can* answer. God, who made us and all things, tells us that we live on. More than that: God became man, died and rose again. In His rising He has given us the certainty of our own.

That's just religion, blind faith. Can't you trust your own senses? Stop swallowing what they hand you, and look!

So we are launched on a discussion. Is it against reason to believe in a life after death? At this stage of the conversation we shall not try to establish more than the objector is able to see. There are deeper reasons, but they are for later. He has asked us to look at what happens, so we shall look. He wonders why we can't see what he sees. Very well, what *does* he see?

He sees what happens to the body. It goes into the furnace at the crematorium perhaps. Or it goes into the earth where it will

> rot to flowers and fruit
> with Adam and all mankind.

Stick to what he has actually seen—namely, the destruction of that in which, when he was alive, the man had done a myriad of observable things—occupied space, walked, stood, sat, ate, gestured, slept, woke, spoke, laughed. But is that the whole man?

What we *see* a man doing is certainly not the whole of his activity. There are all the unobserv-able things as well, and they are the more important things, the governing things. There is his thinking, for instance, and his deciding. No eye has ever seen a thought or a decision, no nose smelt it, no hand touched it, no palate tasted it. Ah, your questioner may answer, the eye can see the decision, the ear can hear the thought. But he is wrong, the ear can hear only the words in which the thought was uttered; the eye can see only the actions in which the decision issued. No ear ever heard a thought, no eye ever saw a decision.

He will have to agree that he never saw the body actually doing either of these things. He *assumes* that it did them; that is, he assumes that there was no other element in man to account for them than that which has just gone into earth or furnace. But it is *only* an assumption. He must stop pretending that he is the plain blunt man using his senses and we the superstitious ones swallowing a dogma. If it was in fact the body alone that did the thinking and the deciding, then he has a strong case. But he doesn't know that, it is simply the probability that happens to appeal to him.

Needless to say, I don't think that we have settled the question of survival. I have only shown that what can be seen happening to a dead body does not settle it. There is plenty of thinking and theorizing to be done.

No one questions—not he, not we—that whatever accounts for thinking and deciding is intimately linked with the body that goes to destruction. But is it *identical* with the body? Above all, does it go to destruction with the body? Christ our Lord says it does not. He tells us that, for bliss or woe, life goes on.

But is it only by divine revelation that we answer our questioner? Have we no theorizing of our own to set against his?

Not as to what happens after death. We know no more about our own selves than he does. But without mentioning revelation we can show him why we are so sure that in living men there is another element at work than the bodily. And we can ask him to think along with us as we consider whether this other element might not only continue to exist without the body, but also go on functioning without the body's aid. In all this there is plenty to talk about.

What you call the soul is so bound up with the body that it is unthinkable that it should go on existing, much less acting, without the body.

This small book is certainly not a textbook, still less a substitute for training in philosophy. With our present question, as with them all, I am concerned with the conversation an ordinary believer might have with a nonbeliever. Aristotle or Aquinas would handle it differently, no doubt. But the questioner doesn't ask *them*. He asks *us*. For about two thousand years the mightiest minds have wrestled with the problem of matter and spirit. We can no more say the last word on it than our objector can. Yet we can discuss it with real profit—not only to him but to ourself too.

On certain elementary facts, we and he are agreed. The outer world comes in through our bodily sense organs—eyes, ears and the rest. This we have all experienced. The sensations are conveyed to the brain. We don't actually catch them at it, but those who have studied our nervous system seem to be unanimous about it. Then something happens which escapes observation altogether. As a result of it, we find ourselves *thinking,* building up a whole structure of thought that is somehow based on what came through our senses. Unfortunately, it is dark to us at which point what the senses transmit and the brain receives and assembles passes into what the mind thinks. It's happening in us all the time, but somehow we seem unable to watch ourselves actually doing it.

What is quite certain is that thoughts, which are the end-product of the process, have none of the qualities we associate with the body. "The thoughts of youth are long, long thoughts," says Robert Louis Stevenson. If you asked Stevenson "how long," he would take it for granted that you were trying to be funny and that you had no gift for it.

Thoughts have no length—or weight or color or smell or taste. They are untouchable. No microscope can make them visible, no audiometer can register them. Scientists can measure the electrical discharges that go with individual thoughts, but these are not the thoughts. When we are deciding, for instance, that courage is more admirable than cowardice, we are not comparing the different electrical discharges that accompany our concepts of courage and cowardice and admiration. Most of us are not even aware we have them. They do not enter into our decision. And we see a gulf between thought and matter that is wide beyond all measurement when we consider not one individual concept but all

that our thoughts contain and produce—ideas, social and economic and political systems, whole universes of them.

So far we and our questioner are agreed. The disagreement is about what accounts for the thoughts. He holds that the matter of the human body has somehow developed to the point where it can produce them. The plain blunt man—you or I perhaps—would say that the body is not likely to produce things with no resemblance whatever to itself, that there must be another element in us with the power of giving birth to such offspring, an element which the thoughts *do* resemble, an element which is as un-material as they are, as beyond the reach of the senses as they are. We call it spirit. And the body could no more produce the parent than it could produce the offspring.

Every living body, human or animal or vegetable, has a life principle, what we call a soul, an element in it by which it makes the body to be alive. Man's soul not only animates his body, that being what soul is for, but because it is also a spirit with intellect and will, it has intellect and will.

I know what his comeback is likely to be. It has been made to me so many hundreds of times: "You can't prove it." And on grounds of mathematical reason you may indeed not be able to establish to his satisfaction, or even to your own (though I do, in fact, think I can to mine), that it must be so. But he will not be able to deny that it may be so. And even if he does not see it that way himself, he can see why *we* do. He can also see why we take the next step: Since our spirit could not have been produced by our body, then it does not owe its existence to the body and therefore need not go out of existence when the body does. Death comes when the body can no longer respond to the life-giving energies pouring into it from the soul: it is a failure of the body, not of the soul. With its animating function suspended, it still has its spiritual powers.

*But, in man as we know him, all the raw material,
so to speak, which the mind uses for its thoughts
comes through the sense organs to the brain.
How will the mind get it when sense organs and
brain have gone to dust?*

You can't simply look up a book and produce
an answer. All you can do is to invite your questioner to think along with you and see how it
looks to him. As we have noted, what the process
actually is by which spirit "reads" the brain—i.e.,
takes over the information gathered, assembles it
and produces thoughts from it—we cannot
clearly see, even in the conditions of our present
life. We cannot expect to see any more clearly
how the mind would function in a new condition
which no one of us has yet experienced. But it is
hard to see why it should not "read" the material
world as well as it now "reads" that piece of the
material world which is the human brain—why it
should not take it straight, rather than filtered
through the body's sense. Why should our knowing mind need a mindless filtering plant?

We have reached a decisive point in our
dialogue and must be very reflective about it. In
every question about what man is and what God
is we are forced to clear our minds about the
meaning of spirit. Long ago, asked by a ques-

tioner to define spirit, I answered that it has no shape or size or weight or color and that it does not occupy space. He answered, "That's the best definition of nothing I ever heard." I had told him what spirit hasn't and doesn't, but not what it is.

Spirit is the being which has no parts. One new to this kind of thinking is not likely even to know what we are saying. We can help him by the contrast with matter. Our bodies obviously have parts. The head is not the chest; the liver is not the heart. But in even the smallest material thing one end is not the other, the top is not the bottom. But in a spiritual being there is no element which is not the whole of it. Two consequences flow from this. The first is that spirit cannot occupy space. Space is the arrangement matter makes to spread its parts in: no parts, no spread. The second is that a spiritual being cannot cease to be itself. What has no parts cannot be taken apart, short of annihilation (which only God could cause and He won't). It can only go on being itself.

Our questioner's real difficulty is the one that kept Augustine from baptism for so long, namely, the difficulty of believing that a being not in space can exist at all. We remind him that the occupation of space requires beings that are divided into parts. And why should dividedness be essential to existence? A being which has its existence and all its powers wholly concentrated in its single indivisible reality must be superior to one which must be forever pulling itself together!

Once this idea has become living in a man's mind, he has crossed the great divide. He is a philosopher, only in embryo still, but something has happened in him that will be his permanently. He will see all reality, from atoms to God, differently. To the philosopher the problem is not how the human spirit can function without a body, but why it should need a body.

But of course only a minority will make the effort to cross philosophy's boundary. God can be known and loved by those who don't. Questions can be asked by those who don't.

When your brain is damaged, you can't think.
How then can you think when you've no brain at
all?

Your questioner may mean one of two quite
different things. There is the permanent damage
to the brain which leaves a man conscious, but
permanently "mentally deranged," not in his
right mind. A man in that state *does* think, but
chaotically. All that comes through the senses is
carried to the brain, which assembles and records
it. There the thinking mind takes over. But if the
recording instrument is damaged, it can offer the
thinking mind only a mess to do its thinking
about.

Or the questioner may mean simply some
temporary bodily damage (it need not affect the
brain directly) which renders a man unconscious
for the time being. This is the more difficult problem of the two. As I said earlier, Aristotle or
Aquinas would answer him more competently.
But the questioner probably would not understand a word they said. I wonder if he will understand you—or me—any better!

Remember, it is not the mind that does the
thinking, it is the man. The mind is what he does
it with, but it is *he* who does it. It is the damage to
him that affects the thinking. And he is not simply

a *spirit* (or mind or soul) which has a *body* that it can use as an instrument. He is a union of the two. He is an embodied spirit or an enspirited body. If *he* is damaged in certain ways he may be unable to function normally either in the mental or the material field.

What immediately survives death is not the whole *man*. One element in him dissolves, rots away. The other element, the spiritual, survives and (until the resurrection of the body, of which we shall speak later) it must go it alone. As we have already seen, our mental activities, even while we still have our bodies, are largely dark to us, though we are experiencing them all the time. And, in any event, we have no reason to think that the mental activities of the disembodied mind will be bound by the same rules. The conditions in which it is functioning will be so very different.

Come back to our damaged man, living but unconscious. Is he a proof the mind cannot function when the body is damaged? Not a proof, certainly—for two quite different reasons, two questions we cannot fully answer.

The first is that the soul has a double function. As a soul it animates the body, keeps it alive and in action; as a spirit it thinks, wills, decides. But it is only one single soul, and if more of its energy is drawn off for the animating of a damaged body, it will have less to use in thinking and willing and deciding. As death approaches, even one who has a lifelong habit of praying finds praying difficult.

The second reason is that we cannot be sure that the mind is not functioning when the man is unconscious. There is one function it is certainly performing: it is holding on to the knowledge it had before the accident. The man usually returns to consciousness with the same mass of knowledge, ideas, plans, guesses, hopes. He was not conscious of them, but they were there. All that we seem to note is that the mind has not gone on working on these, producing new thoughts. But even that is not certain. Unconscious cerebration is something we have all experienced to some degree—a thinking process continuing and problems clarified without our awareness.

All this we discuss with our questioner, but not as laying down the law, with him the student and ourself the professor. We invite him to think along with us. There is so much involvement of brain and senses in the thinking of the embodied spirit each of us is that no one can be blamed for feeling that he just cannot swallow the idea of going on when the body isn't there.

But no sane man holds his own swallowing power as a final test of truth. And even a very

reluctant materialist may admit survival as a bare
possibility after all, one which he is not entitled to
dismiss absolutely. Survival, considered without
reference to what God has told us, may seem to a
Christian anything from a high probability to a
sheer certainty. But God's word is decisive.

*The notion of a being functioning, or even exist-
ing, not in space is sheer verbiage. You can say it,
but you can't see it. Call it spirit if you like. But it is
literally inconceivable.*

"Literally" is precisely the wrong word here.
In this context, its use is illiterate! What the questioner meant to say was that he could not imagine
such a being, which would have been true. The
trouble is that he thought that was what he was
saying. It is a long step toward literacy and so
toward mental maturity to see why he wasn't.

Imagination is the power of making mental
pictures of the material world. Things that the eye
has seen, the ear heard, the body touched, the
palate tasted, the nose smelt, can be reproduced
or recalled in the imagination—either straight, so
to speak, or in any variety of combinations, and in
the recall there can be immense power.

> Odors when sweet violets sicken
> Live within the sense they quicken,

says Shelley. A scent or a tune, recalled as it was
experienced, can storm the emotions. Colors recalled but in combinations nature never knew can
have effects in us greater than we have words to
express. It is a rich gift, imagination—but limited.

What the senses cannot experience, the imagination cannot reexperience. That is to say, it is limited to the material world, the spatial world. The world of spirit is beyond imagination's reach. It can neither affirm it nor reject it.

To say that an idea is inconceivable means that the intellect cannot think it; roughly that there is a contradiction in the idea concealed by the words into which it is cast, a contradiction either in itself, as if one spoke of a four-sided triangle, a contradiction of known certainties as if one said that God was untruthful.

A being—God, say, or the human mind—existent but not in space, is indeed unimaginable. The senses cannot take hold of it; neither the eye in our face nor "that inward eye which is the bliss of solitude." That there is no contradiction in it, I have already tried to show. Both intellect and imagination are necessary; human life would be unthinkable without either. The intellect, the power in us by which we are in contact with reality as known, can be stimulated by imagination. Imagination, ill-nourished by intellect, can have a crazy carnival.

Our difficulty is that imagination works all the time and effortlessly—we just *do* it! For intellect there is "the insupportable fatigue of thought." All too easily we let imagination do intellect's work, either providing us with pictures that seem to answer our questions and make intellect's sweating labor unnecessary or, as in our present question, causing intellect to reject what imagination cannot picture.

THE MIND
OF CHRIST

About survival Jesus had no doubts at all. Dying on the Cross, He promised the thief who was dying alongside Him, "This day you shall be with me in Paradise." A while before He had said to the Sadducees, who did not believe in a future life, "As for the resurrection of the dead, have you not read what was said to you by God: 'I am the God of Abraham, the God of Isaac, the God of Jacob?' *He is not God of the dead but of the living*" (Matt. 22:31-2). So the patriarchs, dead some fifteen centuries then, were alive. And Matthew, Mark and Luke all tell of the Transfiguration of Jesus on the mountain when Moses and Elias appeared and conversed with Him.

Our life does not end with death. That was the context in which His whole Gospel had meaning. That was the good news, the liberating truth He had come that men might have. In what He tells of the judgment, there is survival for *all,* in everlasting joy for some, in everlasting fire for others.

We read this in Matthew's twenty-fifth chapter, when Jesus' own death is close. But He had said it in all clarity earlier. "Do not fear those who can kill the body but cannot kill the soul" (Matt. 10:28). "Fear him who can cast soul and body into hell" (Luke 12:4). As early as the Sermon on the Mount we hear Him telling of the adultery in the heart of a man who lusts for a woman. He

27

goes straight on to say, "If your right eye causes you to sin pluck it out and throw it away. . . ." (Matt. 5:29).

Compared with the endlessness of the life to come, our life on earth is brief—the beat of a gnat's wing, as Mohammed was to say—but it has a formidable finality. "If your hand or your foot causes you to sin, cut it off and throw it from you; it is better for you to enter life maimed or lame, than with two hands or two feet to be thrown into the eternal fire" (Matt. 18:8).

This life is brief, but it is decisive. The self we have formed here, the self in which we die, is the self that enters on the next stage, which has no end. "It is appointed unto men to die once, and after that comes judgment" (Heb. 9:27). The Greek word for judgment is *crisis.* Death is the crisis time.

It seems to me that this life is too short to be decisive in our everlasting destiny. I'm attracted by the idea of reincarnation.

I suppose it's a matter of temperament. I find it repellent. But that's as may be. For the Christian the matter is settled. As we have just seen, the Epistle to the Hebrews (4:27) puts it bluntly: "It is appointed to man to die once and after that the judgment." This fits perfectly with Christ's own account of the judgment. Some go to lasting bliss, some to lasting woe; there is no third category.

It is interesting that there is no reference in the Old Testament to death followed by continuance in another personality. The Israelites must have met people who held such a belief, for in one form or another it is in so many of the religions of India. In one form or another, I say, because it has to be related to the general belief of each religion. Hinduism is not Buddhism.

Buddhism is having something of a revival in the Western World. It holds that the elements of the self are rearranged at death in one "self," one "individual" after another, until the individual vanishes forever in Nirvana (a Sanskrit word meaning "to blow out"). This, of course, is a wholly inadequate account of one of the great world religions. Unfortunately, there is no space here for more. The general rule remains: It is best to find out about a religion from one who holds it.

Do you, a grown man, seriously believe that when you die you will knock on a pearly gate and Peter will take you to the angel who's been keeping your spiritual bank account?

Practically everybody talks about the next life as though it were comical. The comicality of course begins the moment after death: death at least is known to be serious. Catholics are supposed to think that their souls will knock at heaven's gate. (But what will it knock with? Souls don't have hands, they smilingly remind us.) Peter then takes us to the Recording Angel, who adds up all the good deeds of our life and all the bad, strikes a balance and gives us the result: heaven or hell, as the case may be.

When your questioner has made the jokes you've already heard many times and you have politely agreed that they are very funny indeed, the least he can do is listen while you tell him what we *do* believe about what happens at death.

St. Peter doesn't come into it. Our Lord gave him the keys of the Kingdom of Heaven (Matt. 16:19). But the Kingdom of Heaven in the New Testament does not mean heaven; it means God's realm on earth. In this particular case it means the Church. Our Lord had mentioned that in the previous verse. And the giving of the keys did not mean that Peter was to be the janitor. In the ancient world the keys of a city were in the hands of the governor. That we should meet him at the Gate of Heaven is the one thing everyone seems clear about. But do not count on meeting him there. That will happen only if he happens to be passing that way at the time; he has no function there. The keys Christ gave him are at present in the Pope's hands. I do not envy him.

As to the judgment which is to decide our eternal destiny, there is only one question that matters: Have we the Grace of God in our soul? If we have, then heaven is for us. If we have not, then heaven cannot be ours—not because we have failed to deserve it (who could *deserve* heaven?) but because we could not live in heaven without it.

Why does the Church make it all so complicated?
Why not just say that if you're good, you'll go to
heaven; if you're bad, you won't?

Simplicity is not always a virtue—a key might
be too simple to open a lock. The study of any
single area of life—philosophy, say, or psy-
chology—becomes very complicated and we
take it for granted. Religion—studying the relation
of this life, of which we have some experience, to
the life after death, of which we can know only
what Christ has told us—cannot be as simple as
A B C. He wants us to walk in the light, not just to
stumble along in the dark.

So you persuade your questioner not only to
listen, but to listen closely, while you tell him
about Sanctifying Grace, your relations with God.
All living beings have natural life, which gives
them the power to do the things that go with that
kind of being—cows to live the lives of cows,
crocodiles the lives of crocodiles, men the lives of
men. But the power to do things that go with
being men is not enough for life in heaven. It is
not even enough for the life we should live here
on earth.

"Unless one is born *again* of water and the
Holy Spirit he cannot enter the Kingdom of
God," says Christ. Observe Christ's word *cannot*.

By birth we are members of the human race. But that is simply not enough. We must be born again as members of Christ. By birth we have our intellect and our will. By rebirth the intellect has faith, the power to believe what God says simply because He has said it. The will has charity—which is love of God and love of our neighbor—and planted deep in both intellect and will is hope, the certainty that God wills to save us and will save us *if we don't refuse Him.*

Both there and here we need powers to do things which by nature we cannot do. Our natural life just isn't adequate. We need *supernatural* life.

You can't just tell your questioner this and hurry on to the next point. You must help him see it as the reality it is. An example may help him to see what you are saying. By our natural life as men, our lungs can breathe earth's atmosphere. But our lungs could not function in the atmosphere of another planet. We would "die for the want of breath" (to quote a song of my boyhood). To live there we would need new powers of breathing which by nature we do not have. And, just as life on Mars would be beyond the natural equipment of our bodies, life in heaven is beyond the natural equipment of our souls. In heaven we are to see God face to face. Human nature does not equip us for that.

The extra equipment, the *super*natural equipment, is Sanctifying Grace. It is not a passport admitting men to heaven. It is quite literally the power to live there. It is not just a pious phrase; it is as real as lung-power or eyesight. And we must have it on earth, though it will reach its full flowering only in heaven.

Of one person Scripture seems to tell us where he went when he died. Judas, it says, went to his own place. As we read them, these sound the grimmest words ever said of a man. We hope they will never be said of us. But they will. Every one of us will go to his own place. Of this we are assured by that justice which gives to every man his own. It is our knowledge of what Judas had done that makes us fear that he went to hell, that that was his place.

But, heaven or hell, to our own place we shall all go. What makes heaven *any* man's place? The possession by his soul of the power to live there, the life above our nature which heaven calls for, that life of grace of which Christ tells us that the living element is love of God and love of our neighbor. Hell is the place of those who love self to the exclusion of God. But, as it happens, the examples our Lord gives of eternal loss are all related to faults in our love of neighbor.

REFUSAL

Why not drop the cruel doctrine of hell and go back to the simple, loving teaching of Christ in the Sermon on the Mount?

There is an instant answer to the question. In the Sermon on the Mount we find more of our Lord's teaching on the fact of hell than anywhere else in the Gospels.

People generally think of that sermon as ideally short—eight sentences—all beginning with the word "Blessed." If only, they feel, their own parish priest would match its brevity! But the Beatitudes are only the beginning. St. Matthew's setting down of the Sermon occupies three chapters: 5, 6 and 7. It would take about twenty minutes to read aloud. And in it we are warned of hell again and again.

Our Lord tells us that the man who says "you fool" to his brother will answer for it in hell; that if eye or hand leads you into sin, it is better to pluck out the eye or cut off the hand than to enter hell with your body unmutilated; that a broad gate and a wide road lead to perdition. As we hear His threat to some to whom He will say "Depart from me, you that traffic in wrongdoing," we are reminded of the same opening words with a more terrible conclusion: "into everlasting fire that was prepared for the devil and his angels" (Matt. 25:40).

So there is no point in appealing from the Church's teaching on hell to the love of Christ. Her teaching is His. Yet Christ *is* loving. In some way hell can exist and *God* still be loving—and not only loving, but the very self of love. Nothing tests the firmness of our belief in God's love more than the certain fact of hell.

Hell seems to contradict love in so many ways, among them that God should send men there in the first place and that He should keep them there everlastingly, not bringing them in the end to heaven.

It ought not to need saying, yet it does, that we must never treat any question about hell flippantly or humorously, as though we thought eternal anguish funny. We should hold our jests for some topic with less agony in it. We should never treat damnation as a matter of cold logic, as though we were solving a problem in geometry. Triangles don't feel. St. Paul reminds us that the letter of the law can kill (Cor. 111:6).

A believer for whom the thought of hell holds no horror has no business talking of it at all. He can only make his hearers see God as callous as himself. There is one further point: for every one of us damnation remains a possibility. If a man realizes *that* he is not likely to be merely clever about hell.

Our own certainty of God's love may be so strongly founded that nothing can shake it or even touch it. Thank God for that. But we must not therefore write off the questions as trifles or merely be impatient with those who raise them. They mean a great deal to the man troubled by them. Not only that—they mean a great deal in themselves. Many a Christian listening to them in untroubled trust has not really grasped what hell is. I don't mean its horror, I mean its meaning.

"Fire," for instance, as Scripture uses the word, has depths that a box of matches will not account for. "Our God is a consuming fire," says the Epistle to the Hebrews (12:29). "Everlasting" is more than merely on and on without end. But deeper than these, at the very heart of the mystery of damnation, lies the question of why anyone is in hell. What decides? The answer to that involves not only God but the meaning of human life and the fearful power of decision that lies in the human will.

Hell is indeed a contradiction of love. It means love refused. But the refusal is not in God. *It is in the sinner.* It is sheer fantasy to think of God's love as at last exhausted and His justice taking over. Judas, we remember, went to his own place. All men will go to their own place. It may be heaven or hell, but it is their own. God will not force their decision.

*You say the devil is an angel, and therefore far
above us intellectually. But if he is as intelligent as
all that, how could he be fool enough to damn
himself eternally?*

For most people the devil is a figure of fun
with horns, tail, pitchfork, blue fire, invented by
priests to frighten the simpleminded. But those
who realize how frequently he is mentioned in the
New Testament cannot get rid of him so easily.
They reject him as a figure of fun, but only to
preserve him as a figure of speech. What has
happened, they say, is that the tendency to
evil—to wickedness in man and to disaster in the
universe—has been given a name and a personality. For what purpose? To impress the simpleminded, of course.

It won't do. When Our Lord calls the devil "a
murderer from the beginning, a liar and the father
of lies" (John 8:44), He is not talking of a force or
a tendency. He is talking of *someone*—and a
fiercely important someone. He was surely thinking of the serpent of Genesis who lied to Eve,
who passed on his lies to Adam. By that victory
Satan acquired a de facto lordship over the world,
for he had found a weakness in man and with the
superiority of his intellect over ours he could play
on it with deadly effect. Mankind lay fallen under

his princedom in the sense in which Paul could speak of men whose god is their belly (Phil. 3:19). When Christ's redeeming death was at hand, Satan was very much in His mind. Luke tells us that Satan tempted Judas to betray Jesus.

A few days before Calvary we hear Christ say, "Now is the judgment (the crisis) of the world: now shall the prince of this world be cast out" (John 12:51). At the Last Supper He comes back to it twice: "The Prince of this World comes and in me he has nothing" (John 14:30). And again, "The Prince of this World is already judged" (John 16:11). In his first Epistle (3:8) John says, "The reason the Son of God appeared was to destroy the works of the devil."

So our Lord took the devil seriously. How are we to do the same? We begin with the angels, bodiless spirits, all the energy in them going straight into the purely spiritual activities of knowledge and will, none of it drawn off for the animation of bodies. If a questioner says that the notion of such beings is repugnant to the scientific mind, we remind him that none of the natural sciences pretends to show that their existence is impossible or even unlikely since science's realm is matter. If angels exist at all, then, like all other spirits, they are wholly outside the reach or range of what your questioner means by science.

"If they exist at all," I say. Do they? Scripture says they do. And it says that some of them sinned. Listen to what Peter says in his second Epistle (2:4): "God did not spare the angels when they sinned but cast them into hell and committed them to pits of nether gloom." The leader of this group is the devil, Satan (the Abbot of Hell, the Irish used to call him); the rest are demons.

What was their sin? We do not know. Scripture does not tell us, nor does the Church. But a profounder question remains: How, with their intelligence, could they commit any sin at all? Sin means trying to gain something for oneself against the will of God. How could intelligent beings, knowing God's infinity and their own finitude, think they could conceivably gain anything at all against God?

It's mysterious all right. But we needn't go as far as the fallen angels to be puzzled by it. It's right there in ourselves. We know that in any conflict of our will with God's we *must* lose: yet we sin. Intelligence is no sure shield. Even on earth we do what we know will bring misery on ourselves and those close to us.

In other words, sin is in the will, and no amount of intelligence can compensate for wrongness in the will. Much of our own sin comes from the desire for bodily pleasures that the law of

God forbids. Those would not trouble the angels; whatever their sin, it could not be of that sort. It must be a spiritual sin. Their will, remember, was free; they could will to love self more than God. Not that they were silly enough to think themselves God's equals; but in self-love grown monstrous they could resent the superiority in Him which they could not deny—superiority in knowledge and love and beauty, superiority in power above all. They could choose to make their own selves central instead of Him. And that precisely is the sin of pride.

Can we say we know this is what happened? Perhaps. Perhaps not. Certainly there seems no impossibility in it. In the light of its possibility we need not see the existence of fallen angels as unthinkable. And we can see how necessarily their not being in heaven would flow from it. For the whole air and light of heaven is the glory of God. The angels who could love and rejoice in it would stay, now for the first time admitted to see the unveiled face of God as no angel had ever seen it. But those others could only resent it, and no fire can burn like resentment. They might well have found it unbearable. "They forsook their own habitation," says the Epistle of Jude. We may think of God as thrusting them out, or of themselves aching to be gone.

What they could not foresee was that they were going into unending torment, for like every other creature of God they are a mass of needs which only God can meet. But self-fixed in hatred of God, they must get along as best they can with what is left of their autonomy. To turn to Him for relief of their need would torment their self-love more.

Do you really think God is such a monster as to have created as sickening a masterpiece of horror as hell for the everlasting torment of all who do not obey Him to the letter?

What, in fact, *do* we know about the sufferings of hell? There is Dante of course; but he got the general idea and a lot of the details of torment from a book called the *Apocalypse of Paul,* written two or three hundred years after Paul's death, condemned by St. Augustine and never accepted by the Church. It seems also that the nonscriptural writings of the rabbis were sometimes garnished, as many a Christian preacher's have been, with their authors' inventions of what they themselves would do to sinners if they were God. But none of this is God's. Let us concentrate on what Scripture actually has. There is not a great deal of it, and it lacks the lusciousness of Dante and the rest.

What our Lord has to say of hell is linked with Gehenna. In the Sermon on the Mount He says that the man who calls his brother "fool" shall be liable to the "Gehenna of fire" (Matt. 5:22), and the only images we ever hear Him use for hell—worms and fire—both belong to Gehenna. Evidently we must look closely at it. The word is the Greek form of the Valley of Hinnom, which was just outside Jerusalem. Centuries earlier, pagan invaders had used it for an altar to Moloch, with children cast living into the furnace in that unspeakable god's honor. Because of this foulness, the Jews used the place as a vast rubbish dump, with fires always burning to consume the refuse and worms fattening on whatever was edible. The very last verse of the Book of Isaias uses Gehenna as a figure of what happens to God's enemies: "Their worm shall not die and their fire shall not be quenched."

In the ninth chapter of St. Mark's Gospel we find our Lord using that phrase of Isaias. But only for the imagery. It was not the refuse heap of the Valley of Hinnom that He had in mind. Just before His death for the world's redemption He spoke (Matt. 25:41) of the fire in which the lost will be. It is "the everlasting fire *that was prepared for the devil and his angels*"—an earlier fire than that of Hinnom's valley! Revelation, too (20:10), speaks of "the lake of fire and brimstone" into which the devil is to be cast. This is the only use of this particular image of eternal loss by the later New Testament writers, but the Book of Revelation is given to imagery; only there do we find the harps which so occupy the Christian mind on heaven!

Gehenna's fire, like Gehenna's worms, has

the value of imagery; but a fire that is able to torment bodiless spirits is something other. Our minds must not be tied to Hinnom's rubbish dump. It does not tell us the reality of hell any more than harps and pearly gates and streets of gold tell us the reality of heaven. These represent glory; fire and worms represent pain. What pain do they represent?

Upon that the Church's official teaching is as sparing of details as Scripture: fire, torment—that is all it has to say. But it does lead us to see deeper into the reality of hell all the same, for it draws a distinction between pain of loss and pain of sense. Increasingly, the theologian has seen pain of loss—the separation from God—as towering over all else. Go back to Matthew 25:41. The essential suffering of hell is one that men are to share with the devil and his angels. But these are sheer spirits—not even disembodied, for they were never embodied. What suffering is to be common to both them and men? Surely it is contained in our Lord's opening words: *"Depart from me."* For angels and men alike, separation from God constitutes hell.

The hellishness of hell is the loss of God, because God made us for union with himself. He made us with powers to take hold of Him and with needs to drive us to use those powers because only in God can those needs be met. The body needs food and water and without them the man will suffer the torments of hunger and thirst. But the whole man needs God. The need can be masked here on earth by all sorts of substitute interests and activities, but after death it must be faced—this world is left behind and eternity is too endless for substitutes!

All the needs in man that only God can meet will be as clamorous as the body's need here for food and drink; unmet, they will mean anguish. That anguish does not strike the imagination like lakes of burning pitch, but it has its own horror. Why does God not meet the needs and end the anguish? There is a depth of darkness here. One thing is certain, namely men's refusal of God. It is something deeper than particular breaches of His law. The lost are what they are because they have chosen self and will not have God. And self is not enough.

The Apostles' Creed says, "He descended into hell." Scripture says nothing about this.

Actually, Scripture *does* say it. Our questioner does not realize this because the medieval translator used the word "hell." The Latin is *ad inferos,* which means "to the lower places"— anything in the next world lower than heaven. For the translator the hell of the eternally lost was not the only such lower place. There was the "place" where those waited who died in God's favor before Christ's redemptive death opened heaven to the fallen race of man.

The New Testament has a variety of names for it. In the Dives and Lazarus parable, Lazarus goes to Abraham's bosom (Luke 16:22). To the dying thief, Christ calls it Paradise—the word does not mean heaven. On the morning of the Resurrection, Christ tells Mary Magdalen, "I have not yet ascended to my Father." Where had He gone? In his first Epistle (3:19) Peter says, "being put to death in the flesh, but made alive in the spirit . . . he went and preached to the spirits in prison."

It is pleasant to think that those who had waited longest for the news of Salvation were the first to know it had come.

Why don't you drop all the nonsense about heaven, with its harps and hosannas, and hell, with its devils and pitchforks? Why not just admit that you don't know?

Consider an episode that might happen just about anywhere in our world. A group of people are discussing the sudden death of a friend. A banker, let's say; Jones, let's call him. They express their regret with due solemnity. Then we can imagine one of them saying, "Hard to imagine old Jones sitting on a cloud and playing a harp, isn't it?" There are smiles all round.

If there were a Catholic in the group, it would not occur to him to make the comment, for he would know that heaven does not mean sitting on a cloud and playing a harp any more than hell means sitting in a furnace and being prodded by a devil. Nor would he think it funny when someone else said it. For the humor lies in the suddenness of the transition from yesterday's occupation, banking, to today's occupation, harping, and the Catholic would allow for the possibility of purgatory in between. After the cleansing there, Jones would be a different man—his employers would probably not recognize him (and certainly would not employ him).

But the average man has no views on purga-

tory and only the fuzziest uncertainties about
heaven and hell. I don't mean the straight unbe-
liever, for he will admit nothing after death. I
mean a whole mass of people who would certainly regard themselves as Christians. As we
have noticed, they never talk of the life after
death save jestingly. "Heaven for climate," they
will say, "hell for company." That is their way of
saying that hell is too hot, but all the really interesting people go there—only saints and such
are in heaven. Actually, it is their way of not
thinking about the next life at all.

That they should prefer not to think about hell
is easy enough to understand. But why do they
switch their mind away from heaven as well? I
think the reason is that they know only the scrip-
tural imagery of heaven, nothing else. Of whatever their more believing grandparents may have
known, all that has filtered down to themselves is
a confusion of pearly gates, clouds, golden harps,
hymn-singing—what our questioner sums up as
harps and hosannas. But not a word about the
reality of man's relation to God there. They
haven't a notion of the plain fact that in heaven
we will at last be fully human and not merely
the rough sketches that we are here of what men
and women ought to be.

So they see heaven as a spectacular church

service. They no longer like church services. The prospect of one that goes on forever is more than they can face. Certainly it is no compensation for the sins they must give up to make sure of getting there. Hell likewise suffers from imagery and nothing else—imagery drawn this time not so much from Scripture, which does not let itself go on that subject, but from Dante, to say nothing of Milton. The theme was taken up into a thousand pulpits, with each preacher licking his lips as he added torments of his own invention. There was no attempt to explain why the sinner was there, except that he had sinned once too often and had achieved the impossible: he had exhausted the infinite mercy of God.

But that infinite mercy is *inexhaustible* because it is infinite. The lost soul is refusing a mercy that is never exhausted. And the real pain of hell is not this phantasmagoria of red-hot pitchforks but in the loss of God. Our questioner, and the millions he speaks for, have never heard any of these truths, least of all the last of them. The loss of God is hell's essence, just as the living contact with God is heaven's. To leave God out is not to know the first thing about either heaven or hell.

Left with nothing of hell but the tortures of the damned, men could see God only as hateful—if they took them seriously. Rather than hate God they have decided to treat them as a joke. To that extent, they have made the better choice, for it is better to be wrong about hell than wrong about God, and seeing Him as hateful is the limit one can reach in being wrong about Him.

But it is desperately important to be *right* about hell. At the end of the road of life, it stands as the place of failure, an appalling possibility for every one of us. But what is it? What is failure? And what about the inexhaustible mercy of God?

*Why should anyone be condemned to an eternity
of pain for a few hours of sin? Couldn't they be let
out after they've served a reasonable term?*

There is a basic misunderstanding here and it
cannot be rooted out by a few well-chosen words.
Settle down for a careful discussion of what saves
and what damns. No one is in hell because of this
or that sinful act or because of all his sinful acts
together, just as no one is in heaven because of
his virtuous acts, singly or in total. He is in heaven
because he loves God and his fellowmen, or he is
in hell because he doesn't. What decides is the
state of his will, what fundamentally he loves.

Christ says that we must keep the commandments, but they are simply the application of the
two key commandments: love God, love your
neighbor. Practically all the evils that Christ
speaks of as incurring damnation are for failures
in love of neighbor. Men do not get an eternity of
bliss for a few hours of virtuous deeds but for a
love of God and men that is settled and abiding.
They do not get an eternity of pain for a few
hours of sin but for a love of self issuing in a hate
of God and contempt for others that is settled and
abiding.

Can we spell this out for ourselves in any
comprehensible way? If we could see the depths

of our own soul it would be easier, for the decision we are considering is not on the surface. We follow our own experience as far as it will take us and simply theorize as best we can about what lies between that and the ultimate refusal of God which makes hell possible.

That we can choose to do God's will, even though we may be aching with desire to do things He has declared evil, is a fact of experience. That we can choose to refuse God's will and seek our own satisfaction against it is also a fact of experience. We really *can* grab the immediate pleasure and damn the consequences, even knowing what the consequences are. We can swing toward God and away from God. But with most men one direction tends to become more or less settled. There can be deviations and even reversals, but the general direction shows itself pretty clearly. We will to do God's will or we will to do our own. For a man to do the second of these is quite simply to treat himself as his God, making his own will (or wish or appetite or mood) the law he lives by, in a universe he did not make! All this is a matter of universal experience.

We can hardly have *experienced* the next stage, yet there seems no impossibility in it—and in *its* possibility is hell's. We conceive a man growing in self-love, a beginning of self-deification—the true God not necessarily denied, but disregarded. We conceive self-love grown monstrous in him, self not quite *seen* as God but *served* as God, the true God resented for His omnipotence—in other words, for being God. Suppose a man did die in that condition, with love of self swollen monstrous and God hated in consequence. What could God do with him? Heaven would be impossible, for heaven means total contact with the God he hates. What is the alternative? To carry on his existence without God, refusing everything from God but existence, the one thing it is not in his power to refuse (indeed, would self-love let him refuse that?).

Of one result we can be reasonably certain. The man we have been describing has chosen self, and self is insufficient. His deepest needs cannot be met from within his own self, so there is anguish from needs unmet, comparable vaguely with hunger for bread and thirst for water. What this anguish is we do not know and can but theorize: frustration, emptiness, despair. Again, one thing seems certain, that to his anguish from needs unmet is added the anguish at his own inability to meet them. He has made self into his god and his god has failed him. He lives in the awareness of his own futility. Futility is hell's atmosphere.

But he clings. There is no question of release. His suffering lies in his refusal of God. While he continues to refuse, there is no end to it.

These notes were written for believers. But Christ's command of love applies to all men, even to those who are not conscious of any particular belief in God. They can have a real sense of right and wrong transcending their human tendency to serve self. They can have a real response to the needs of others; that is, they can have a genuine love of others or they may see others merely as means to their own self-serving. If there is any real love in them we know that love cannot be lost eternally. Men have cost Christ too much for Him to let them go lightly.

How much chance of salvation has the ordinary man? Christ says, "Many are called but few are chosen" (Matt. 22:14). What are the odds against my being among the winners?

But it is not a sweepstakes or lottery, where only a handful can possibly win and the overwhelming majority must lose. Your chance of salvation or mine is not limited by the number of winning tickets available. There is no element of competition at all. There would be joy among the angels if everybody won. Each is judged by the use he has made of the gifts God has given him.

What then did Christ mean? Was He saying that only a minority would be saved? Definitely not. When He was asked the direct question (Luke 23:13), He did not answer. The "few" and the "many" in the text are an example of a Jewish way of speech, the use of an exaggeration to make sure that listeners got the point.

We do it ourselves, when, for instance, we say, "It's raining cats and dogs." Everyone realizes that we mean that the rain is unusually heavy. So when Christ spoke of the many and the few His Jewish hearers would make a necessary allowance for emphasis. He was giving a warning—and the purpose of a warning is to warn! Had He said that not all who are called are chosen, it would have been precise but might have passed unnoticed.

Christ wants every man to be saved, for He has paid a great price. He will do anything to help us do the right thing, but *we* must do it. Nor will He pretend it is only a formality. It is deadly serious. Only a bad doctor would not emphasize, or overemphasize, what the consequences to the patient would be of not obeying his orders. That surely is why Christ said in the Sermon on the Mount, "The gate is wide and the way easy, that leads to destruction, and those who enter by it are many" (Matt. 7:14).

His point is not the rarity of salvation, but the effort we must make. We cannot be saved without Him, but He cannot save us without us, so to speak. We cannot just lounge into heaven.

As to the judgment which is to decide our eternal destiny, only one question matters: Have we the grace of God in our soul? If we have, then heaven is for us. If we haven't, then heaven cannot be ours—not because we have failed to deserve it (who could *deserve* heaven?) but because we could not live in heaven without it.

Even if you're right in saying that men can refuse
God once and for all and so doom themselves to
suffer in what you call hell, it still remains that
God could free them from suffering by annihilat-
ing them. Anyhow, why does He create men who
He knows will go to hell?

Your questioner—like most Christians, like
yourself, I imagine, like me certainly—finds the
endlessness of hell's suffering all but unbearable.
If only there might be an end to it! In the third
century, Origen, the most powerful intellect the
Church had known since St. Paul, seems to have
felt that at the end salvation would reach all
(though not Satan!). And we never totally dismiss
from our minds the "All shall be well" that the
fourteenth-century English mystic Julian of Nor-
wich tells us Christ said to her.

But how? If the main suffering of hell lies in
needs which only God can meet, then if souls
continue to hate God, it is hard to see how the
needs can be met and the suffering cease. It is
harder still to see how they can be brought into
the living contact with God in which heaven con-
sists.

All this our present questioner sees. But he
sees *annihilation* as a way out and *non-creation*
as a way of not going in. We remind him, and
incidentally ourselves, that we have no clear light

on any of this. We are certain of the love of Christ; we are certain of the existence of hell. But as to how the one can be reconciled with the other we can only speculate, sometimes seeing a gleam of light, sometimes a tantalizing possibility that light might be there if we could but strain our eyes an inch further. Always there is the awareness of all that we do not know even about the human will, and over all the mastering fact that God is love. From the love of God nothing must separate us.

Do we get any gleam upon annihilation as a way out? Not very much, certainly. God will not annihilate, we know: "These shall go into everlasting punishment, but the just into everlasting life." But why doesn't God put the damned out of their misery? Doesn't mercy demand it?

Here we may find that all is dark. Yet I find myself wondering. If the damned were offered annihilation, would they want it? Forget about the boiling pitch and the fiends with red-hot pincers. Hell is not like that. There is emptiness, frustration and rage, all eating at the lost, wrapping them in bitterness. But they must have found some sort of modus vivendi. Might their self-love be of such an intensity that they would refuse annihilation, clinging to the self they have made their god, their world well lost for love, self-love?

If that were a possibility, it would help as an answer to the second of our questions: If God knows a man will go to hell, why does He create him? Why not leave him uncreated? Just what is meant by the certainty that a nonexistent man *would* be damned if he *were* given existence is hard for the imagination to cope with.

We imagine God as seeing all that a given man *would* do on the way to damnation: the lives he would affect, the woman he would marry, the children he would beget, the sins he would cause others to commit. Then we try to imagine God as slicing him out of existence before he could begin: finding another husband for the woman, another father for the children (unless of course their existence is to be canceled along with his). All the lives he would ever have affected would have to be different. So interwoven are we that it could not be simply a matter of pulling out one thread. It would mean a ceaseless arranging and rearranging by God, myriad direct interventions at every instant. And what if, at the end of all things, it turned out that the damned would still rather be than not be?

But all this is fantasy. We have a natural tendency to think we could run the universe better than God runs it; but that is baby-think. We simply do not know what is involved in running a universe. We keep firm hold on the fact that the one who does run it has given the ultimate proof of His love for men. We leave it to Him.

Hell, then, is for those who have made the final refusal of love. What of those who die loving God and loving others, yet with too much self-love, self-indulgence, still in them?

ACCEPTANCE, BUT—

There's nothing about purgatory in Scripture.
The Catholic Church invented it.

Be wary when an objector says that some
doctrine or practice of ours is not in Scripture—
wary of accepting his statement, still warier of
producing texts to prove him wrong.

Scripture does not contain a large-scale map
of the next world from which purgatory is omit-
ted. The knowledge of what follows death was
not instantly revealed to Abraham or Moses. It
grows slowly as Scripture itself grows, with the
passing of the centuries. It has not finished growing. There are strange references in Scripture
which we may not clearly understand to states of
the dead which are neither heaven nor hell, and
such texts as are usually quoted to establish purgatory's existence turn out to be not as compel-
ling as we might wish.

The New Testament was written within a
teaching Church. The Apostles had been com-
manded to teach the whole world all that Christ
had taught them. But we cannot find set out
anywhere in the New Testament the great mass
of truths thus entrusted by Him to the Apostles.
The Apostles went on teaching it and their suc-
cessors do to this day. But we shall nowhere find
it set out in writing. The men who wrote the

Gospels and Epistles gave some of it, but always in the full consciousness that the new Christians had already been instructed in it. The Gospels give a selection of what Christ did and said, with each writer choosing the elements needed for the portrait he was drawing. The Epistles were for the most part written as the occasion arose—some point of doctrine was being misinterpreted, perhaps. Thus one cannot argue from the silence of the New Testament that any particular doctrine was not being taught. Purgatory for instance!

We shall do best if we invite our questioner to think about death—death and himself. The body, by slow wearing out or sudden disaster, is no longer capable of responding to the life-giving energies the soul has been pouring into it from the moment of conception. So it breaks up, rots. But the body was the life-receiving element, not the life-giving one. What does the life-giving element, the soul, do?

"Goes to its own place." We have already noted that the phrase, used of Judas in Scripture, applies to all men, though "its own place" is not the same for every soul. That depends on what each man profoundly loves. As we have seen, those who love self as against God get self, with God excluded, which is the very essence of hell. Do the rest go to heaven?

The notion that one might be not bad enough for hell, but not good enough for heaven, has probably never occurred to our questioner. God's judgment is not a matter of putting a tick or a cross against every soul. Souls, at death as in life, may be at either extreme—total rejection, total love—or at any level between. One thing Scripture says which Catholics seem to have taken more seriously than others is that we are called upon to be perfect. "Be ye also perfect," says our Lord, "as my Heavenly Father is perfect" (Matt. 5:48). We must be perfect in our humanity as God is in His divinity. Give your questioner a rough reminder of what the self may be like at any given moment: clutching at what we want, evading troublesome duties, excusing ourselves all too easily for the ways we have hurt others, resenting the way others have treated us. No, he will not think of himself as perfect at that moment.

Perfection means loving God with our whole mind, soul and strength and our neighbor as ourself. Ask your questioner if he feels that this is a reasonable description of himself *at that moment.* And, if not at *that* moment, why at the moment of death?

When Christ tells us to be perfect, He is stating the ideal. But He knows us too well to think that most men can score 100 percent. A passing mark is a good deal lower than that.

You now administer your shock; or rather, the Book of Revelation, our Apocalypse, will administer it for you. The description of heaven in chapter 21 (do please read it) ends with the words, "Nothing defiled shall enter." There is no question of a passing mark. We must be wholly clean. Small sins, committed without reflection and forgotten too quickly for repentance, are still imperfections, defilements. Worse sins, deadly sins, repented of quite sincerely, yet not sufficiently, with no intensity in the sorrow to match the evil of the sin, hold us this side of perfection. They dim total purity.

At this point the objector will certainly say that you are splitting hairs. A man, he will tell you, either *is* sorry or he isn't. Persuade him to think again. We may very well be sorry for having done wrong, wish we hadn't, feel rather sick with ourselves, yet be letting ourselves off pretty lightly. Actually, we do sometimes experience intense contrition over wrong we have done to a friend and mentally scourge ourselves for treachery or ingratitude. But how rarely we feel like that about sins against God, to whom we owe everything.

Fullness of sorrow really does cleanse the soul, whereas sorrow that, while quite sincere lacks its due intensity, may remove the guilt of sin yet leave something needing remedial treatment—a debt not quite paid, uncleanness not wholly removed, the defect in us which caused that sin not healed.

If "nothing defiled shall enter heaven" were the last word, after which there is only silence, we might well despair. But for the uncleannesses still present in those who die loving God, the Church teaches that there is, by God's mercy, cleansing. Note the very word the Church uses, purgatory—not penalty—the soul made clean, purged of every last trace of the uncleanness which defiles.

Even if your objector is not convinced, he will at least see what you mean and he will have seen deeper into himself than is perhaps his custom.

How can the pain of purgatory make souls any cleaner?

We have considered the statement in Apocalypse 21:27 that nothing defiled can enter heaven. We are now ready for the other side of this truth, namely, that no one defiled would want to enter heaven—provided he knows what heaven is. For the life of heaven involves a total contact with God, a total awareness therefore of His all-purity, which would make any defect in ourselves unbearable (somewhat in the way in which damaged eyes cannot bear strong light or a damaged digestion strong food). The more the soul loves God, the more intolerable God's direct presence would be. Every instinct would make the soul want to hide itself and its uncleanness. We remember how Peter reacted to his first realization of Christ: "Depart from me, O Lord, for I am a sinful man." He loved Christ, but suddenly could not bear his own unworthiness in His presence.

What is the nature of the uncleanness that keeps out of heaven souls who genuinely love God and for whom all bliss would lie in being with Him? We have already had some discussion of this, which must be summarized here. Love decides our eternal destiny, and love is in the will.

Sin is self-will as against God's will. By repentance the will surrenders to the total goodness of God; but insufficient repentance, contrition inadequate to the gravity of the refusal of God involved in the sin, still leaves a taint of unsurrendered self.

The love of God is genuine, the desire for God genuine, but neither is perfect. And perfect we must be. When the sorrow for sin is total, justice has no more claim on the soul. No punishment it could inflict would bite more deeply than the soul's own sorrow. And selfishness has no hold, for the will is wholly united at last to God.

That, insists your questioner, is all very beautiful, but what has fire, a word your spiritual writers are fond of, got to do with it? St. Matthew told us of our Lord's speaking of the fire that was prepared for the devil and his angels. Hebrews 12:29 speaks of God himself as a consuming fire. I have never actually counted the references, but I have a feeling that fire is almost as common in Scripture as water, and with as great a variety of meanings. Both can be destructive, both can be cleansing. As cleansing, fire means suffering, accepted at God's hands.

Again and again I have known objectors to move closer to agreement than is normal with them by being shown the relation between suffering and the cleansing of the soul. Sin is the thrust of the will to what we want against what God knows is right. By its very nature the acceptance of suffering makes for the correction of that wrongful thrust, for the will takes to itself precisely what it does *not* want because it sees the will of God in it.

We cannot pretend to know what the suffering of a disembodied soul is, but for the souls we are considering there can be no question what the principal element is. They long to see the unveiled face of God, yet they could not bear to see it while any uncleanness remains in them. They suffer from the anguish of their desire and the clear vision of the taint of self still in their own will. By accepting God's will, they find healing for their own will. Christ's blood, shed on Calvary, was always available for the cleansing of their iniquity. The acceptance of God's will removes what in them resisted the cleansing action of Christ's blood—the greed that clutched or the sloth or cowardice that evaded, the resentments for wrongs suffered by us, swallowed up in the total understanding which is at the heart of forgiveness.

When the cleansing is complete, they are at last fully human. The evil they have done is purified and they can face God and both those who have wronged them and those they have wronged.

Why do you pray to get souls out of purgatory? You call it a place of cleansing. Do you want them out before they are clean?

If purgatory were simply punishment, there would be no problem in praying for the release of souls suffering there. We would be asking God in His mercy to write off the balance of their sentence. But, as we have noticed, the Church calls it purgatory, not penalty. To purge is to make clean; cleansing is primary.

In the soul there may be some uncleanness, some defilement, something of self-will not wholly surrendered to God. We have seen how the acceptance of God's will and the pain involved in the acceptance does by itself heal the last traces of defect: the soul is ready for heaven, where "nothing defiled shall enter" (Apoc. 21:17). So we seem to be asking God to take souls out of purgatory before suffering has completed its cleansing work. It sounds like praying for a patient to be released from the hospital before he is cured.

Stated like this it sounds ridiculous. Yet we begin to see the answer. After all, if a friend is in the hospital we *do* pray for his release and there's nothing irrational about that. We are not praying that he be sent out unhealed, but for his speedier healing. Are we asking for a miracle of God's power? Certainly we are, if he can't be healed without it.

Apply this to purgatory. The pain souls suffer there is for their healing. It is the pain of the will making the ultimate effort to bring self into that total acceptance of God's will which is perfect health—and perfect freedom. Whether or not we fully realize it, we *are* praying for a miracle. A damaged leg can be healed by a miracle if God chooses; so can a damaged soul. And if God *does* remove the weakness in the soul which prevents the total union with Him that it longs for, He is not contradicting free will. On the contrary, it's the way the will is longing to go.

So we offer our prayers and such sufferings as we may have, technically called our merits. And not only to move God to help a soul toward perfection, *but to put at His disposal that with which He helps it.* I find it very hard to state this clearly, but the whole of our religion is based upon the mysterious fact that in the spiritual order, as in the material, the strength of one can help the weakness of another. In the natural order it looks simple enough. We can see the strong man communicating his strength, the wise man communicating his wisdom, the learned man communicating his knowledge. But how does

God apply the strength of one man to the weakness of another, the sufferings of one man to the self-will of another, the merits of one man to the healing of another?

How God does it is God's secret. But that it is so has been revealed to us. Listen to St. Paul (Col. 1:24): "I make up in my body what is wanting in the sufferings of Christ, for His body which is the Church." We have noted before the widespread habit of reading Scripture or listening to it in a state of pious coma. By the text I have just quoted, if we are fully awake, we shall be stunned twice over. It is startling enough to hear St. Paul speaking almost casually about something lacking in Christ's sufferings, even more startling to hear him say that his own sufferings may help supply the lack!

What is Paul saying? What our Lord did in his own self lacked nothing; it is what He does in and through *us* that falls short—because we do. Yet it is part of God's redeeming plan that our merits, joined with Christ's and lifted into the power of His, should also serve. We are not meant to be simply spectators at our own redemption, with ourselves doing all the sinning and the sinless Christ doing all the suffering. His sufferings were a kind of healing stuff which God could apply to men's souls. In union with His, ours can be so too. Without His, ours would not serve the redemption of the race. But without ours, His cannot reach as far as they might.

Your questioner may find all this difficult. I find it so myself. But at least one thing should stand out clearly: In praying for the souls in purgatory, we are not asking that the cleansing process should be stopped halfway through. We are using, with more or less comprehension but with total trust, the certain fact that our prayers can speed the cleansing.

MATURITY

The Church tells people about the joys of heaven in order to make them willing to put up with any amount of exploitation here on earth.

History will not bear this out. In the social-economic sense, nothing has been so revolutionary as Christ's message. Before His coming, proletarian revolutions were practically unknown. In Christendom they were practically endemic. When they spread to the non-Christian world they occurred most often where His message had been heard and usually in terms of it.

All the same, heaven as the carrot on the donkey's nose became a rallying cry for the Left. It received its classical formulation in Joe Hill's song about the answer a preacher will give if you ask him for something to eat:

> You will eat by and by
> In that beautiful land beyond the sky.
> Work all day, feed on hay,
> There'll be pie in the sky when you die.

When this was written, around the turn of the century, it may have had at least an appearance of plausibility. But it has precious little now. How often do you meet anyone who is excited at the thought of the joys that await him in heaven or even gives them a thought?

If I had to sum up the crowds I have talked to on street corners in the last forty years, I would say that practically nobody wants to go to heaven. I don't mean that I myself am at this moment anxious to leave this world and be on my way to the next. But all the same I do see heaven as a place of great joys. Most people apparently don't. The reason is the one I referred to a little while ago: the only idea of heaven most people were brought up with was of sitting on a cloud, playing a harp, shouting Hosanna. All this sounds like a sort of super-technicolor church service—poor compensation for all the sins they feel they will have to give up if they want to get there. But this idea is precisely *not* an idea. It is simply a series of pictures in which a Jewish mind of long ago tried to make vivid the realities of heaven. Unless one knew the realities already, one would not get them from the pictures. And it is the realities that make heaven worth striving for.

But with the determination of everybody either to be silent about heaven or comic about it, how is one to find out what the realities are?

Fun indeed is what men have when talking about heaven. There was the man who asked a speaker in Hyde Park, "Are there toilets in heaven?" Was the questioner unable to bear the thought of eternity without a wall to write on? Or was he just having fun? The speaker answered, "There will be toilets in heaven only if there is waste matter to be eliminated, as to which I have no information."

Unbelievers at all levels have entertained themselves about heaven. We have just mentioned the labor leader Joe Hill, around the turn of the century. Then there was Mark Twain who, in *Letters from Earth* (published fifty years after his death), took the line that the whole and only thinkable activity of heaven must consist in endless sexual intercourse. People more seriously religious than he had hit on a similar general idea. In the myths of Near Eastern paganism the gods and goddesses are sexual maniacs. And the Koran has bodily sex as part of heaven's joy for the saved—allegorically perhaps: the liquid-eyed houris may have been as much figures of speech as are the harps, found only in the Book of Revelation, which have filled so much of the Christian picture of eternal happiness. And it would be a pity not to mention those early Christians who gave up their wives in the hope of receiving a hundredfold in heaven.

Heaven for climate, but hell for company.

Here we have one last example of the way these vast matters of heaven and hell are turned into jests and so flipped out of the mind's consideration. We have already glanced at it. It is a kind of pendant to the cliché that saints are good people and martyrs are those who live with them, which in Ireland I heard as "His wife's a saint, God help him."

The sheer endlessness of this jesting has created an atmosphere in which Christians find themselves apologizing for their own acceptance of Christ's plain teaching. They have come to accept the certainty that eyebrows will be raised if their secret should come out in conversation.

Upon this notion of hell for company, as it happens, we do get a gleam of light from Scripture: when Christ was about to cast out the demons in Gerasa they begged not to be sent back to the abyss which was their home, they preferred pigs' bellies (Luke 8:31–32).

Since the issue of the company has been raised, what will it consist of in heaven? Hebrews (12:22) tells of "the heavenly Jerusalem, city of the living God: here are gathered thousands upon thousands of angels . . . here are the spirits of just men made perfect: here is Jesus the spokesman of the New Covenant."

In the previous generation, a standard pulpit phrase was "the road to hell is paved with good intentions." I do not know who first said it, but it made good sense. To me one of the signs of change in the spiritual weather came with my first hearing of the parallel phrase, which we shall consider next.

*The road to heaven is paved with lost oppor-
tunities of enjoyment.*

The intent was different, but there was sense
in this one too. It pointed to a flaw in the Church's
care for souls. For who expects to *enjoy* heaven?
What idea have we been given of any joy in
heaven to compensate for the pleasure of all the
sins we have had to give up in order to get there?
Yet, it is what life here is all about, what salvation
is all about.

We have been told of the Beatific Vision, the
direct seeing of God in heaven. But, as most of us
learnt it, there was not much promise of enjoyment in the presence of God for *us*. It was too
technically theological, not easy to relate to the
selves we are accustomed to being! One could
not avoid the feeling that some less glorious eternity would have suited our commonplaceness
better; something with beef and beer in it
perhaps, or the wine and women we are told
Mohammed promised. "The tedium of personal
immortality"—that phrase of Karl Marx's friend
Engels—can touch a nerve in us. We cling desperately to such joys as we have known, shrinking
from the fullness of human maturity which Christ
shows as the meaning for us of heaven. But can
we get any hint of what that meaning will mean?

In our present immaturity can we get any insight into the maturity that is to be ours if we do not refuse it? It is worth trying.

*The world of Jesus was different from ours. What
has He to offer the persons that you and I actually
are?*

We can know about heaven only what we are
told. What God has not revealed—i.e., unveiled
to us—we cannot know, not even if we are
Mohammed. The first key to understanding is in
Christ's words to the Apostles at the Last Supper:
"I go to prepare a place for you, that where I am,
you may be." They may not have felt much
instant consolation in that. It had to be lived with,
grown into. By the time Paul wrote to the Corinthians it had come alive to the point where Paul
could find himself wondering if he would not
choose to die sooner in order to be with Christ
sooner.

If we are to feel like that, Christ must be
immensely real to us. He wants our company.
But honestly, do we want His? A teacher wrote to
me of asking a class of Catholic teenagers if they
would like to have Jesus in class with them. They
decided they would not: He would be too
goody-goody. He would object to too many of
the things they liked doing—smoking for one
thing, having sex for another.

It is important that we should not fool ourselves about our feeling for Christ. It is only as we

get to know Him better, and ourselves better, that
we can share in the richness of Bach's "Jesu, joy
of man's desiring." Yet even that is only a first
step. To see heaven as companionship with Jesus
is a beginning of understanding; but it is not
heaven's ultimate depth. The mere thought
would have horrified Him. He was the Way, not
the Goal; His justification for existence was to
bring us to the Father: "No one comes to the
Father but by me." He had come, He says, that
we "might have life and have it more abun-
dantly." So heaven means life, life with the
Father. But what does *that* mean? Knowing ourselves as we are, do we find it saying anything to
us at all? Does it link with anything in our experience of being ourselves?

The New Testament uses one single verb for
the life of heaven—uses it three times. It is the
verb "see."

Jesus speaks of "angels who see the face of
my heavenly Father continuously"—that is to say
they never cease seeing Him. Their seeing Him is
a basic fact of their life there, as breathing is of
ours here.

St. John uses the same verb of us: "We shall
see him as he is" (1 John 3:2).

St. Paul too uses it of us in that thirteenth

chapter of his first Letter to the Corinthians, which seems to me the charter of the Christian life. "Now we see as in a mirror dimly, but then [that is when perfection has come] face to face" (I Cor. 13:12). Pause upon this. The mind's seeing is what we call knowing; it is the mind's primary way of entering into possession of reality. According to the truth and depth of our knowing is all else that we do. Any defect in our knowledge—the things we don't know, the things we know wrong—affects our emotions, our imaginings, our decisions, our loving above all.

We hardly need Paul to remind us of the inadequacy here on earth of our seeing, our knowing and our loving, not only of God but of just about everything. We constantly come up against our ignorance, trip over our errors, fail those who love us. God above all we see "in a mirror, dimly." We do not see Him as He is but as He is "mirrored" in His works, including the work He does in ourselves. As we grow in understanding of His universe and of ourselves who are made in His image; as we listen to what He has told us of himself; as we use our minds on the experience of living by Him, we can develop a richer and fuller idea of Him. Yet we are still seeing Him in a mirror, less dimly but dimly still.

Left to ourselves we might assume that in

heaven our idea of Him would grow to its ultimate rich fullness. St. Paul says no. Even that
would be too little. We shall see Him face to face,
in direct gaze.

Linger a while on this "seeing" which is not
the "seeing" with the eyes in our face, but with
the mind—knowing, in fact. What do we mean
when we say we "know" someone? The intellect
is what we know with. But actually, we do not get
that person himself into our intellect. What we get
is a whole bundle of ideas about him—that he is
American, say; intelligent, musical, industrious—
all this accompanied by a sort of mental picture
by which we recognize him when he is there and
remember him when he is not. As we get to know
him better we multiply our ideas and refine them.
He is intelligent? Yes, but stupid about some
things. Kindly? Yes, but not in the early morning.
This is what we call getting to know him better.
But it is always by means of the ideas that we
know him, not by directly possessing his actual
self.

All this may sound either too obvious to be
worth saying or too airy-fairy to be worth bother-
ing about. But we shall not grasp the meaning of
heaven without it. We may love God here upon
earth; we may have our minds filled to overflow-
ing with the thought of Him, but it is still by means

of the ideas we have managed to gain that we know Him. In heaven we shall know Him *direct*. He himself will have taken the place in our mind of the idea we have of Him here on earth. It may seem like a verbal trick to say that in heaven we won't have an idea of God. But it is precise. We'll have no need of an idea. What would be the use of an idea when the intellect possesses the Reality itself and knows it for what it is? God will be known, says St. Paul, with the directness with which He knows us; seen, says St. John, as He is. Seeing Him thus *as He is* we shall see the Son too, and the Spirit who proceeds from both—the Trinity in whom we were baptized, whom we have seen so dimly here below.

One can see why it has been called the Beatific Vision—the seeing which makes us blissful. Our knowing power will be in direct contact with God who is infinite goodness. Every element in our being will be at last wholly fulfilled, functioning at its highest upon the Highest.

If you are as excited about all this as I am, it will be depressing to hear your questioner say, "Is that all?"

In my experience that is what he always does say—the first time. So we start all over again.

What do you have to say about Christ's life in heaven?

What Revelation, the last book of the New Testament, has to say of heaven is worth careful reading. It gives glimpses of depths beyond our mind's reach, especially in the relation of the Lamb, which is Christ, to the One who sits upon the throne, who is God but whom we meet only as a Voice. The book is less a teaching than a series of ecstasies. I shall be content here with the Gospels and Epistles, which present their teachings more accessibly, though there's often ecstasy too.

To Mary Magdalen on the morning of His Resurrection, Christ says, "Tell my brethren I am ascending to my Father and your Father, to my God and your God." Forty days after, He rose into the sky till a cloud concealed Him from His followers. He had given His Church into the keeping of the Holy Spirit.

What is He doing in heaven?

In its ninth chapter Hebrews says, "He entered Heaven on our behalf"—that is, to do something for us. The seventh chapter (verse 25) tells us what the "something" was: He is making intercession for us. "He holds his priesthood permanently . . . consequently he is able at all times to save those who draw near to God through him, since he lives on to make intercession for them." In other words Christ, priest forever, is offering himself, once slain on Calvary, now forever living, to His heavenly Father in order that what He won for our race should be made their own by all the race's members.

We see Mass as a reflection of this. The priest, in the name of Christ and by His command, offers the same Victim to the same Father for the same purpose, and we offer with him. When the saved arrive in heaven they may well find themselves joining in Christ's archetypal Mass! After all, they are members of His body and as members they will not have to search for it.

You say the Beatific Vision means the seeing that makes us blissful. It makes me yawn.

We talk of seeing God face to face, of our whole self in direct contact with the Supreme Being. And the people we talk to look blankly back at us, seeing in all this nothing they can recognize as joy.

They wonder if they could stand it forever and ever. They wonder if God might let them have an occasional holiday from so much bliss, a holiday in which the pleasures they now know could console them for the aridities of life in heaven. So, we have found Mark Twain saying that sexual ecstasy is the one thing that would make eternity tolerable!

This sort of reaction is natural enough. We may sometimes have found ourselves hoping that heaven won't be as inescapably spiritual as all that! But of course we are fooling ourselves. We are exactly in the position of a small boy who cannot imagine why grown-ups waste their time on poetry or science or girls and ignore the space suit and the cowboy outfit that are such bliss to himself.

We pass from stage to stage of development and our powers and interests and pleasures change. The man who insists that what gives him pleasure now is the only kind of thing that ever will is assuming that he will be eternally retarded. To see heaven as barren if it lacks the delights of the present moment is to refuse to grow up. We laugh at the small boy with his space suit. Mark Twain and his sexuality are just as funny.

In our growing up here on earth, we realize that each stage is a mystery to the one before it. The big boy cannot convey to the little boy what pleasure he finds in girls; the grown man cannot convey to the big boy what pleasure he finds in metaphysics (or whatever). St. Paul, quoting Isaias, says of the life God has prepared for us, that eye has not seen it, nor ear heard it, nor the heart of man in any way imagined it. But, though we cannot imagine what life in heaven will be like, we do know certain things about it and we can use our minds on them most profitably.

Back now to the feeling already mentioned that something a little less perfect would suit us better, that heaven seems to call for a sort of person that we just aren't! Glance again at the small boy rejoicing in his space suit. He is puzzled by his big brother, who goes to work, earns money, could buy any number of space suits but doesn't buy even one and spends all his money on girls. Observe that the big brother can understand the small boy's excitement over the space suit, for he has been a small boy himself. But there is no way in which the small boy can understand what his brother sees in girls. That belongs to a level of development he has not reached, calls for experiences he has not had. There is no way in which those on earth can grasp the actual experience of life in heaven.

All this talk of Beatific Vision sounds like nothing but Words! You can hypnotize yourself with them, but they don't mean anything to me.

The objector we have just been considering couldn't see any joy in looking straight at God. This time the difficulty lies in seeing what St. Paul—and Jesus and John—were actually saying. It is very much in the mood of the heckler who called my definition of spirit the best definition of *nothing* that he had ever heard.

After all, St. Paul says that none of us have seen the life God has prepared for us, nor can we possibly imagine it. Why, says the questioner, can't you just leave it at that?

St. Paul did of course say it. He was quoting Isaias. And Paul, because he had concentrated so long on Jesus and at such depth, knew more about the next life than Isaias and did *not* leave it at that.

It is true that we have no experience to tell us what the experience can be of seeing God face to face—seeing Him not by an idea of Him richer than any saint or theologian ever had here, but himself seen as himself by direct gaze. But we do know what seeing and knowing mean in our own relation to reality, and they will be perfected when we reach maturity, but not denatured.

Each new truth known enlarges our world, widens it, deepens it. The decisions we make are sounder for our knowing more. The things we enjoy, we enjoy better for knowing them more truly. Every power we have is strengthened: the power to love, especially, which is decisive of our human quality. That applies to every piece of truth we learn. But God is supreme truth and the mind's total possession of Him means total maturity, our will wholly harmonious with His, love therefore at a new level. Joy will be at a new level too, for the surest joy known to us is to have our powers in action upon an object worthy of them.

All this, we may feel, is only words, inadequate to infinite reality, saying nothing to our finiteness. Yet there is light in them, not darkness only. We know ourselves enough to know that sin will be impossible—not because our wills will have lost their freedom: free will does not mean that the will is free to want anything that it does not see as *in some way* good for us. But once we have seen Father and Son and Holy Spirit "face to face" nothing contrary can have any promise of good in it.

Our intellect, I think, can make some sense of the idea of every element in ourselves functioning at its best on supreme reality. Yet, we may find it hard to see where joy comes in, or any likelihood

of warmth at all. We feel we would welcome
something nearer to our own mediocrity. (Like a
man I knew who went to a seminary but was back
with us in a month. "Too many bloody prayers,"
he explained.)

Heaven indeed can sound like a Church service: endless singing of God's praise; surely God
himself must be sick of it! But those in heaven are
more continuously aware of God's splendor than
we on earth are of the weather! The natural reaction in the depth of their being, whether or not it
finds words, is continuous. Adoration is their way
of life, the context in which all their other activity
takes place.

MATURITY **111**

Doesn't all this theologizing about heaven add up to daydreaming?

Believers in a world to come almost automatically figure it in terms of the joys they have known here on earth and this can easily mean wishful thinking or daydreaming. We should make real use of the mind on what Christ has in fact told us.

On one thing He leaves no doubt: the life that follows death is a continuation of our life here; the self—that in each of us which says "I"—is the self as it has been hammered out, by life and by us, when death finds us. Christ says that if eye or hand or foot leads us into sin, it would be better to pluck out eye, cut off hand or foot, better to enter life with one of each than be cast into hell with two! (Matt. 18:8).

He was speaking figuratively, but what He was saying is frighteningly clear. We are not to be merged in God like a drop in a boundless ocean. I will always be *I*. What I have made of myself will pass on to the next stage and that stage will last forever. Death is the crisis (remember, the Greek word means judgment).

On what shall we be judged? On what we love. The commandments list ways in which we fail in love, but Christ says that love of God and love of neighbor are their life-principle. If we die loving self to the contempt of God and man we

shall get self and nothing else. Scripture does not show Satan or the demons as tormenting those who have refused love. That belongs to Dante's phantasmagoria and a thousand years earlier to the fictional *Apocalypse of Paul* (of which Aquinas thought so little). The essential torment of the lost—as of Satan—lies in the futility to which self-love grown monstrous has doomed them.

Nothing defiled shall enter heaven, says Revelation in its next to the last chapter. As we have seen, this is a working out of Christ's own word: you are to be perfect as your heavenly Father is perfect. We are not to be infinitely perfect, naturally. We are to be all that we as human beings ought to be, as God is all that God ought to be.

But even thus reduced to my scale, the phrase frightens me, as does Revelation's application of it. As I write this paragraph I know that I am not perfect. The mere notion that here is no element of defilement in me, no element that needs cleansing, would be laughable. If I died this moment, if anyone dropped dead at any moment, how fit would I or he be for the all-purity of heaven? For the life of me I cannot see how most of us can enter heaven without some sort of cleansing after death. And "cleansing" is all that the word "purgatory" means.

"I don't want to take off my body" (so said a child dear to me, after a sermon on death).

Purgatory or not, the soul arrives in heaven without its body. The body will not rise at once. There will be a period in which the soul will go it alone. This, we are told, is because of man's sin. My own theory about this is that it is not simply a penalty for sin, but a way for the spirit to recover from sin's effects. Here on earth the body has usurped an improperly dominating position in the human compound, with imagination governing both our seeing of life and our decision-making. The spirit of man needs a period on its own, so to speak, to grow into the habit of using the powers which it had allowed to slip from it. We do not, I imagine, grow in one act into the habits of heaven. When the spirit has rediscovered and grown into the use of its own primacy, it can safely be reunited with the body.

Meanwhile,

> John Brown's body lies a-mouldering in the grave
> But his soul goes marching on.

That has become a drinking song. But in its odd way it enshrines the truth Christ uttered when he said to the thief dying on the next cross, "This day you shall be with me in Paradise." We find it difficult to imagine the soul doing anything even in heaven without the body. But, as we have seen, to a philosopher the spirit's dependence on the body here below is a greater difficulty. And, anyhow, it seems worthwhile to remind ourselves that until the separation of souls and bodies is ended there would be very little for the senses to function on in heaven: only Christ's body and His mother's, which are quite beyond our present picturing. Otherwise, the disembodied soul's heaven will be as wholly spiritual as itself!

The soul is the element in the human compound which does the knowing and the willing and the loving. It continues to do all these things in the disembodied state. So we ask the saints to pray for us, confident that they will not love their fellowmen less now that they are living in the presence of the God who created men in His image, in the sight of Christ who died for them.

But the separation can be only temporary. Without the body we would lose part of our raison d'être. Pause upon this. There is a universe of spirits and a material universe. They would be two separate universes if man by belonging to both did not join them into one. Man is not just a superior animal or an inferior angel. He is the priest of the unity of creation.

The resurrection of the body is impossible. If a man is buried, the worms divide his body among themselves. If he is cremated, what is left to be brought back to life?

There are few problems that excite an audience so much. I was once asked what if a man is eaten by a cannibal, the cannibal eaten by a lion, the lion by a crocodile—I've forgotten what happened to the crocodile. (I rather think he ended up as a lady's handbag.) All these giddy imaginings are based on the idea that what we get at the resurrection is the identical body, reassembled.

Believers in the resurrection have made the same mistake. At what age shall we rise again? As we were at death, or in our prime? There once was a belief among the pious that we shall rise at the age of thirty-three, that having been worked out as the age at which Christ died.

But that is *not* what the "same" body means. The scientists tell us that there is not a single cell in my body that was there twenty years ago. The cells go on so many years (I've forgotten the exact number) and are replaced. Time has eaten more bodies than all the carnivorous animals. Yet it is not nonsense to say that my body continues all through my life. Its identity derives not from the matter assembled in it but from its animation by the same spiritual soul—and that soul will animate my risen body.

The body's continuing identity is mysterious enough even in this life. It is not more so in heaven. It has been theorized that there may be some element attached to, and surviving with, the soul which is its link with the matter of the body.

In interviews with Dr. Moody, reported in *Life After Life,* many of those who returned to life after being declared clinically dead spoke of having left the body and watching it from somewhere outside it while it was still being worked on by doctors. But they were aware of having something they felt to be a body—but different. Naturally, it has been suggested that this is the "link" I have just mentioned. Who knows? Their accounts have a verbal similarity to St. Paul's (2 Cor. 12:2) of his being caught up to the third heaven: "whether in the body or out of the body I do not know, God knows."

Your risen body doesn't sound much like a body to me.

For Christ's risen body and our own, it is well to make a careful study of the fifteenth Chapter of Paul's First Letter to the Corinthians.

With soul and body reunited, we shall be the same self, yet surely not very recognizable! Take one phrase from that chapter— "the perishable in us already perished, the physical body made into a spiritual body." Our nearest and dearest left on earth would not know us. Shall we feel like strangers to ourselves? Shall we have anything but memory to assure us of our continuing identity? The change will be immeasurably greater than that from caterpillar to butterfly. It will be immeasurably greater even than in our first great change, the change from the womb to the outer world, and more startling, because we shall know about knowing, as the newborn infant does not.

Take Paul's phrase "the perishable stripped away." Whatever in our earthly self is relevant only to the condition of life here will be gone from us. Thus Christ tells us that death, which is the gateway to the next stage, will have no further function since the stage we enter at death is forever. "Our mortality," says Paul, "will have put on immortality." In this we shall be like the angels.

For us, as for them, there will be "no marrying or giving in marriage." Man is made in the image of God, a piece in a mosaic, complete when the race is complete. God the Son is the image of God as it can be produced in the divine nature; the whole human race is the image of God as it can be created of nothing. Marriage is for the continuance of the race, and the race will have achieved its completion. There is of course no hint that mankind will not still be male and female, or that the difference will be meaningless or joyless.

Man will still be man, nothing that is essential to our humanity will be lost.

I make all things new (Rev. 21:5).

We have already discussed the newness in our mind, seeing God direct, God taking the place in it of the idea of God which was the best we could do in this life. It is the full flowering of the supernatural life into which, here on earth, we were born in Christ.

The body will have its newness too. "The Lord Jesus Christ will change our lowly body to be like his glorious body" (Phil. 3:21). So our risen body will be as wholly part of our perfection as Christ's was of His—when suffering had brought His to it. Paul calls it a spiritual body, which sounds like a contradiction in terms. Certainly we cannot know what it will be like. But at least the spirit will be wholly in control as, but for sin, it always would have been.

There will be neither inertia nor rebellion in the body to diminish the perfection of their union. The body will no longer draw spirit downward to its own mindlessness or to its own natural subjection to the ceaseless flow of time. For the spirit there will be no distracting awareness of moments flowing away. As Christopher Dawson says it, "Matter will be the extension of spirit not its limit, the instrument of spirit not the enemy."

We have already spoken of mankind's unique

priesthood as the link between the spiritual world and the material. That surely will continue, as Hebrews tells us Christ's own mightier, priestlier priesthood does. The material universe continues too, at a new level of being—new heavens and a new earth. In the vision of Revelation (6:14), "the sky vanished like a scroll that is rolled." We find the same simile in Isaiah (34:4). Given the language of prophecy, this need not mean that the earth we know and the heavens we know will be annihilated, only that they will be profoundly and rendingly changed. In Revelation (21:5) we hear the voice from the throne cry, "I will make all things new"—not all new things, so to speak.

Here below the Christian is a new man, which does not mean that he is another man altogether. He is the same man with a new vital principle operating in him, as faith, hope, charity and the rest. In heaven the new man will have reached maturity. Similarly, it seems the heavens and the earth will have a new energizing within them, producing effects of which we as yet have no knowledge. But Paul gives us the essence of the change: "[God's] plan for the fullness of time is to unite all things in Christ, things in heaven and things on earth" (Eph. 1:10). "The creation itself will be released from its bondage to decay and obtain the glorious liberty of the children of God" (Rom. 8:19).

With each of its members made new, humanity will be wholly new. We shall be joined in a community of knowledge and love with our fellowmen such as we have never known here. For just as the goal of each individual is to grow to full perfection as a man, so the goal for the human race is to grow to full perfection as a community. In organic union with Christ, humanity will mirror the perfect community of Father, Son and Holy Spirit, in whose image we are all created.

So there, if we do not refuse, we shall be, with a spirit made new, and a body made new, in a universe made new. Can we make anything of it for our mind's refreshment in a world which grows daily more chaotic?

What the experience will be, we have no experience to tell us, save in an occasional gleam or glimpse. It is amusing to speculate, but no more than that. We say, perhaps, that we shall talk to Shakespeare and Socrates, rather as a small boy talks to his elders about what he means to be when he has grown up. One thing we can be sure of: even Engels could not find it tedious. As, I hope, he now knows.

*It's magnificent, I admit, but it still doesn't sound
very enticing.*

"Enter into the joy of the Lord" (Matt. 25:21).
Once again, what expectation have we of joy in
heaven? For a great number there is the expectation of reunion with those they have loved on
earth. What else? Do we switch our minds away
from heaven, simply hoping that it may turn out
better than it sounds? Christ told the Apostles, "I
go to prepare a place for you, that where I am
you may be." How conscious are we of that?
What delight do we see in being with Him, "seeing him as he is." Are we longing for the moment, as Paul was?

We have smiled at the atheist mockery of
heaven as pie in the sky. But Christ does indeed
tell of a banquet to come. There is the parable of
the king who gave a wedding feast (Matt. 22).
There is His promise at the Last Supper: "I shall
not drink this fruit of the vine till I drink it new with
you in the Kingdom of God." And Luke gives us,
"I appoint for you that you may eat and drink at
my table in my Kingdom" (22:29).

But the "Kingdom of God" in the New Testament normally means the Church. My own feeling is that the banqueting, the wining and dining,
the beefs and fatlings, refer to newness of life on

earth following the descent of the Spirit. I feel this not only because marriage feasts seem not to belong in heaven, where there is "no marrying or giving in marriage," or because eating and drinking suggest waste matter to be eliminated, which does not fit with our picture of life in heaven. After all, Christ did eat and drink with the Apostles after his Resurrection (Acts 10:41) and Revelation tells mysteriously of the marriage of the Lamb with the Church, a marriage which, like Christ's priesthood, is forever.

All the same, it seems clear that the banquet and the wine to be drunk in the Kingdom of God and the sitting at table with Christ belong to this world—especially as the last words are followed by, "You shall sit on thrones judging the twelve tribes of Israel."

Yet again, does it really matter? The Kingdom of God, which is the Church on earth, is made in the image of heaven, much as man is made in the image of God. "Image" is God's formula at all levels, practically His signature. In the Church as in man the image may be marred and mutilated. But image each is. If Christ uses the figure of a banquet in speaking of the Church on earth, the same figure will have richer application in heaven. For, after all, the main joy of food and drink is not in the nourishment. Paul said wine was good for

Timothy's stomach, of course, but it also "makes glad the heart of man." And, in any event, the main joy of a banquet is in the company. One remembers the people one sat next to long after one has forgotten what one ate and drank. In heaven the company is the point. We have seen what that company is.

But missing from the company may be some we loved on earth. If they are among the lost, how can we not grieve? How can God's own joy be undimmed? We simply do not know the answer to either question. It does seem that we have attached too simplistic a meaning to "there shall be no tears." Heartlessness belongs neither to God's infinity nor to man's maturity.

*How can anyone be happy in heaven knowing of
the suffering in hell?*

Needless to say, no heckler would leave it at
that. There are such obvious ways of sharpening
a point already piercing enough. There is the son
whose mother is lost eternally. There is the friend
whom we once led into sin, with oneself repen-
tant and saved, the friend dying unrepentant.
How can the saved be happy in the awareness of
all that unending misery. How, indeed, can Christ
be happy? Or His heavenly Father?

I have heard no answer that satisfies the questioner. I have heard and read "answers" that
seem to me merely sickening. We simply do not
know, simply have not experienced either the
happiness or the misery. As I have said, our in-
terpretation of "There shall be no tears" may
have been oversimplified. A man to whom the
suffering of others or the memory of his own sins
meant nothing at all would be insensitive beyond
belief. Who does not care what happens to the
beings made in the image of a God wrapped in
His own infinite perfections? We find no evidence
in Scripture.

We are out of our depth. The certainties are
that no finite love can equal God's, that no
human being has ever suffered more for sinners
than Christ did.

But what will it really be like?

There is no way of silencing that question, in ourself or in any believer, be he a great saint or the greatest sinner. It asks itself, and if you have read the fifteenth chapter of I Corinthians you will have met St. Paul's answer: "Don't be silly!"

We shall at last be complete men and women, not just the raw material which God and life are trying to hammer into maturity.

But as to what that maturity will be like when it is at last ours, we cannot, literally *cannot,* know till we have not only reached it but grown into it. Summarizing Paul's line of thought, one who has known only seeds can have no idea of a rose, just as one who has known only caterpillars can have no idea of a butterfly. And the changes in our very selves will be vaster than these. There is no way in which the actuality of the experience can ever be conveyed to us till that experience has become ours.

God's ways are indeed unsearchable, yet we can grow by searching. "A man's reach should exceed his grasp," says Browning. He was not at the moment talking about heaven, but he *did* go on, "or what's a heaven for?"

What shall we *do* in heaven? It can hardly be the goal of all Christ's redeeming and man's striving that we should enter into an endlessness of blissful stagnation. Here, our speculating has less to go on—less, but not nothing.

As we have heard, there will be new heavens and a new earth, a Hebrew way of saying a new universe. To repeat: Just as the new man we are to be does not mean annihilation of the man that we have been and replacement by another, a stranger to us, so it would seem the new universe will not mean annihilation of the world we know and its replacement by another that is wholly unrecognizable. After all, God looked upon the first one and found it good. In man and universe newness means a new vitalizing principle set working by God in what was already there.

Will this revitalizing include animals and trees? Who knows? One can let one's imagination ride on a loose rein, especially about the survival of animals. I find my own mind constantly returning to Christ's word about the sparrows (Luke 12:6): "Not one of them will fall to the ground without your Father's will" (Matt. 10:29). "Not one of them is forgotten before God." He gives this as a reason why we should have no fear of being lost eternally. If he means only that God is aware of the sparrow's death, it is hard to see what reassurance there is in that for us. But if he is telling us that the sparrow is still in the hand of God—as we are—one could go on like this for a long time.

However it may be about animals and trees, the new heavens and the new earth will hardly be mere scenery, a stage setting and no more, a backdrop lending color to an existence just too bodiless without it. God would hardly revitalize a backdrop! Man has an organic connection with earth. Whether in terms of evolution or in the literal sense, he is made from the earth. Earth is the mother from which the creative power of God produced us. However odd a new-made material universe on the far side of death may seem to us, we would live a kind of amputated existence without it, cut off from a root of our being. The universe affects us in a hundred obvious ways, and surely in profounder ways unsuspected by us.

It will continue then, and we shall continue to have both an organic relation with it and a duty to it. For man was created not merely to fill the earth but to till it, to help it to its full fruitfulness. What this will mean in concrete terms we have not been told; nor is there any way of conveying it to us in our present immaturity. What it cannot mean is stagnation.

A Reflection

Whoever has read as far as this knows how I see death and what it opens up for us.

But how do I *feel* about it?

Relaxed!

Death itself, apart from the pain that might precede it and the punishment that might follow, does not bother me. The small girl (dear to me) who didn't want to take her body off was expressing the view of the theologians that the separation of the soul from the body means a rending of the personality from which we shrink. But I haven't the imagination myself to feel the shrinking.

I wonder who does? Most people, surely, fear nothing so much as the loss of the pleasures they have known in the body and the extreme improbability of their continuance: heaven has a chilly feel. That was a rare man whose idea of heaven was eating pâté de foie gras to the sound of trumpets. Commoner is the thought expressed by the seventeenth-century poet Andrew Marvell:

> The grave's a fine and private place
> But none I think do there embrace.

For many a century before Christ, many a millennium perhaps, that was the established view—survival a misery of mere existence. So the Old Testament Jews felt; so felt the great Greeks.

But not I. Christ has told us that He has gone to prepare a place for us, that where He is we may be. His word of welcome when we arrive there will be "Enter into the joy of my Father." Is the detail of the joy beyond present comprehension? I should hope so. I don't want to stay retarded at my present level.

But God will be there, at last seen with direct vision; Christ will be there and his Mother and all who have not refused Him. For those I have loved here I shall have a love with no dross in it: the joy I have had in them here I shall have there, unclouded.

There is one small matter peculiar to myself. I have written so much about the Trinity: Will the sight of Father, Son and Holy Spirit make me wish that I could get back to earth and tear that writing all up? I also feel a special uncertainty about meeting St. Augustine, whose Confessions

I translated. I can only hope he thinks better of my translation than I do. But perhaps by now he may think his own book pretty bad, and my translation not much worse.

I know, for I have seen, that as death approaches, there is a diminishing of the flow of energy from soul to body, a loosening of the bond between them, an unease that can give rise to real anguish. I hope that when that time comes a priest will be there to hear my sins and in Christ's name absolve me and give me the Blessed Eucharist (which the Church pleasantly calls *viaticum,* supplies for the journey) and anoint me, anoint especially the senses through which from the beginning of life the world has poured in on me.

But with all this, I can't conceive a future life without a possibility of cleansing (which is what the word purgatory means)—not because I deserve it, but because I need it. The thought of entering the presence of the all-pure God as the spotted object that I am revolts me. There are the elements of self unsurrendered—me still wanting what I want just because I want it. Healing is a better word than cleansing. My will needs straightening; and that cannot be done without pain—not penal pain, pain in the sheer forcing of the will away from habits grown into second nature. Here or hereafter, with God's aid I must will my own will straight. He will help me to do it. But He won't do it for me.

I hardly ever meet anyone who wants to go to heaven. I do. Yet not at once. Not today. Next week, perhaps.

So there *is* a shrinking. Clearly I am a puzzle I have not completely solved.

This book was set in V.I.P. Souvenir at the DEKR Corporation, and it was manufactured at Offset Paperback Mfrs., Inc. The book was designed by Joseph J. Vesely, who also supervised its production.